Monster Seaweeds

The Story of the Giant Kelps

Mary Daegling

P **DILLON PRESS, INC.**
Minneapolis, Minnesota 55415

Library of Congress Cataloging in Publication Data

Daegling, Mary.
  Monster seaweeds : the story of the giant kelps.

  (Ocean world library)
  Bibliography: p.
  Includes index.
  Summary: Discusses the largest and fastest growing
plant in the ocean, which serves as a home for countless
sea creatures, is a source of many chemicals, and is a
valuable food for human beings.
  1. Giant kelp—Juvenile literature.   2. Giant kelp—
California—Juvenile literature.   3. Kelp bed ecology—
Juvenile literature.   4. Kelp bed ecology—California—
Juvenile literature.   5. Kelps—History—Juvenile liter-
ature. [1. Giant kelp.   2. Kelps.   3. Kelp bed ecol-
ogy.   4. Ecology] I. Title.   II. Series.
QK569.L53D34 1986   589.4'5   86-13591
ISBN 0-87518-350-6

Dillon Press, Inc., 242 Portland Avenue South
Minneapolis, Minnesota 55415

Printed in the United States of America
  2 3 4 5 6 7 8 9 10 95 94 93 92 91 90 89 88

Contents

Giant Kelp Facts 5

1 The Importance of Kelp 9

2 The Kelps as Algae 19

3 Underwater Forests of Giant Kelp . . 28

4 A Home in the Sea 37

5 Kelps through the Ages 48

6 Kelps, the Source of Algin 55

7 A Trip on a Kelp Harvester 62

8 The Mystery of the
Disappearing Kelp 70

9 How the Weather Affects the Kelps . . 81

10 Kelp Farms of the Future 92

Appendix A: Learning More About
Giant Kelp 103
Appendix B: Scientific Names for
Sea Animals 105
Glossary 109
Selected Bibliography 116
Index 118

Acknowledgments

With grateful appreciation to Wheeler J. North, Ph.D., and Howard A. Wilcox, Ph.D., for their knowledge and their willingness to share it; and to Donald Conner, Manager; Ronald H. McPeak, Senior Marine Biologist; Charles Adair, Captain, retired; and D. Craig Barilotti, Ph.D., Marine Biologist, all of Kelco Division of Merck & Co., Inc., for their time and their cooperation; and to James Folsom, Assistant Curator, Huntington Botanical Gardens; to Richard J. Rosenthal; and to Steven K. Webster, Ph.D., Director of Education, Monterey Bay Aquarium, for their assistance; and to Gary E. Davis, Research Scientist of the National Park Service, and to John J. Grant, State Marine Sanctuaries Coordinator of the California Department of Fish and Game, for their thoughtful suggestions.

Photo Acknowledgments

The photographs are reproduced through the courtesy of: Charles Arneson—cover, 8, 42, 78; the California Institute of Technology and U.S. Navy—63, 94, 97; Floyd Clark—71; Ronald H. McPeak, Senior Marine Biologist, Kelco—57, 59, 66-67; Museo Nacional del Prado—51; Dr. Wheeler J. North, Professor of Environmental Science, California Institute of Technology—38; Pacific Gas and Electric—82; Richard Rosenthal—11, 12, 15, 21, 22, 26, 29, 30, 33, 41, 44, 45, 47, 76, 87; Steven K. Webster, Director of Education, Monterey Bay Aquarium—25, 74; and Dr. Howard A. Wilcox, U.S. Navy Oceans Systems Center—93. Cover: an underwater view of a giant kelp bed off the coast of southern California.

 *Giant Kelp Facts*

Scientific Name:

    Macrocystis pyrifera

Type of Plant:

    Biggest of the brown algae (seaweeds)

Size:

    Up to 200 feet (61 meters)

Rate of Growth:

    Under good conditions, can be 24 inches (61 centimeters) in 24 hours

Requirements:

    Water temperatures between about 45°F (7°C) and 75°F (24°C)
    Sunlight
    Clear ocean water
    Moderate wave action
    Adequate nutrients

Value to Ocean Life:

    Part of ocean food chain; provides habitat to countless sea creatures

Value to People:

Kelp ashes used as fertilizer; minerals taken from kelp include potash, soda ash, iodine, and algin; kelp used as food in many countries

Future Plans:

Giant kelp could be raised in sea farms that would float on ocean currents

Fish swim among giant kelp plants near the Santa Barbara Islands off the coast of southern California. (Charles Arneson)

The Importance of Kelp

Giant kelp is the largest seaweed in the ocean. Under good conditions, it can grow to a length of 200 feet (61 meters)—two-thirds as long as a football field. Giant kelp also grows faster than any other plant in the ocean world. When these king-size seaweeds grow close together, they form huge kelp beds.

A kelp bed has a major effect on the ocean around it. It provides food and shelter for countless sea creatures. It also offers them shade from bright light, or a safe place to hide. A kelp bed softens the action of ocean waves, making the water calmer close to shore.

More than 650 **species*** of seaweeds grow along the coast of California. Among them are more than 10 species of kelp. Their common names often describe how they look—giant kelp, bull kelp, elk kelp, and feather-boa kelp. In Europe, other kelps are known as "wrack" and "tangle." This book will deal with the largest of all—giant kelp.

*Words in **bold type** are explained in the glossary at the end of this book.

A Valuable Natural Resource

To most people, a kelp bed may not be beautiful. It looks like a tangle of messy brown weeds at the surface of the sea. It isn't easy for a swimmer, or even a boat, to enter a thick kelp bed. Surfers prefer ocean beaches that are not cluttered with seaweed. No one ever chooses to have a picnic right next to a pile of smelly kelp washed up on the sand. Fishermen never like seaweed to tangle up their lines, and yet they know they are sure to find fish near a kelp bed.

Even though kelp sometimes gets in people's way, it has always been a valuable **natural resource**. The earliest harvests of all were probably made to gather food for human beings. At times, chemicals from kelp were used to make soap, glass, and even explosives. Kelp is the world's only source of **algin**, a useful natural chemical. Algin is used in more than 300 different products. Algin prevents ice cream from freezing into bad-tasting ice crystals. It makes toothpaste smooth, blends cement mixtures together, suspends the color evenly in printer's ink, and keeps car polish well mixed. It suspends tiny bits of chocolate all the way through a glass of chocolate milk. People use products that are improved with algin every day of their lives.

From above the water, as in this aerial view, the tangled canopy of a giant kelp forest appears to give no hint of the rich marine life below. (Richard Rosenthal)

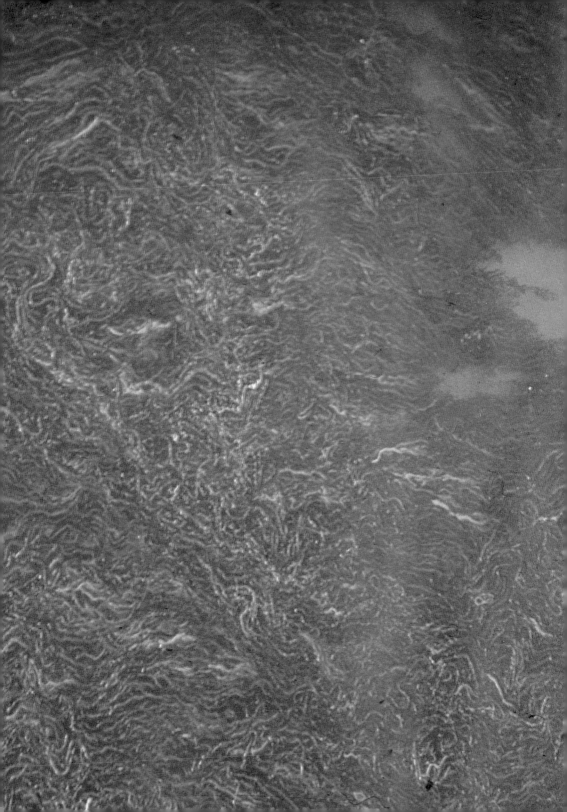

However, human use of kelp is not the only measure of its value. Kelp plants play an even more important part in the great **food chain** of ocean life.

A Link in the Ocean Food Chain

Everything that lives in the sea, or anywhere else on earth, requires **energy** to stay alive. Almost all of the energy on earth comes from the sun. Plants capture the energy they need from sunlight. The kelps need sunlight, too, even though they grow underwater. Plants change this **solar energy** into chemical energy, which is used to build sugars. These sugars can be changed into other substances for the plants' growth and energy storage. This set of processes of capturing light and building sugars is called photosynthesis.

The name photosynthesis describes the process well. The word itself means "to put together with light." Photosynthesis supports almost all life on earth, including our own.

Because kelp plants grow to the surface of the ocean, they reach sunlight that has not been dimmed by passing through seawater. Kelps produce a huge amount of food in the sea. Abalone, other smaller snails, sea urchins, and some kinds of fish feed

Near the Santa Barbara Islands, giant kelp plants grow toward the sunlight shining through the surface of the sea. (Richard Rosenthal)

directly upon kelp. These animals are called **herbivores** because they feed only on plants.

Some creatures depend on kelp in another way. They use it as a **substrate**, a place where they attach themselves and settle down for life. These animals do not eat kelp—they only hang onto it. Because they filter their food out of seawater that flows through the kelp beds, they are called **filter feeders**.

Seawater Soup

To filter feeders, seawater is soup. All the food they ever eat is floating in the water around them. Seawater is often full of food, but much of it is too small to be seen without a microscope. Called **plankton**, this food consists of millions of very small plants and animals, some **microscopic** in size. Floating free, plankton feeds all sizes of sea creatures.

Small particles of plants such as the kelps also add food to the ocean food chain. Bits and pieces of kelp break away as older parts of the plants wither, die, and decay. This material that crumbles off is called kelp **detritus**.

Some filter feeders strain plankton and kelp de-

Many sea animals live among the giant kelp forests. Some feed upon the kelp plants, while others attach themselves and settle down for life. (Richard Rosenthal)

tritus through bristles or fine hairs in their bodies. Others are free-swimming fish that stay near a kelp bed, facing the current with their mouths open. Yet another group of filter feeders traps specks of food on sticky parts of their bodies.

In contrast to herbivores, **carnivores** are animals that feed upon the flesh of other creatures. These meat-eaters come to kelp beds in order to hunt plant-eaters. In turn, the carnivores are eaten by still-larger **predators**. In this way the energy that kelps take from sunlight is spread, in time, all the way through the ocean food chain.

A World of its Own

A kelp bed creates a small world of its own in the sea. The animals that live there depend on kelp, and the plants themselves are affected by the ocean water around them. All of these things, living and nonliving, influence each other. Together they create the **kelp ecosystem**. It is a place of great energy in the life of the sea. Nothing exactly like the kelp ecosystem occurs anywhere else in the ocean.

The famous scientist Charles Darwin noticed how important the kelp beds were 150 years ago. In his journal, *The Voyage of the Beagle,* Darwin wrote:

> "June 1, 1834....The number of living
> creatures of all Orders, whose exis-
> tence ultimately depends on the kelp,
> is wonderful....On shaking the great
> entangled roots, a pile of small fish,
> shells, cuttle-fish, crabs of all orders,
> sea-eggs, star-fish, beautiful...crawl-
> ing...animals of a multitude of forms,
> all fall out together....if in any coun-
> try a forest was destroyed, I do not
> believe nearly so many species of ani-
> mals would perish as would here,
> from the destruction of the kelp."

It is hard to imagine life in the sea without the
presence of giant kelp. If anything should ever destroy
these monster seaweeds, the ocean world would lose a
resource of great value.

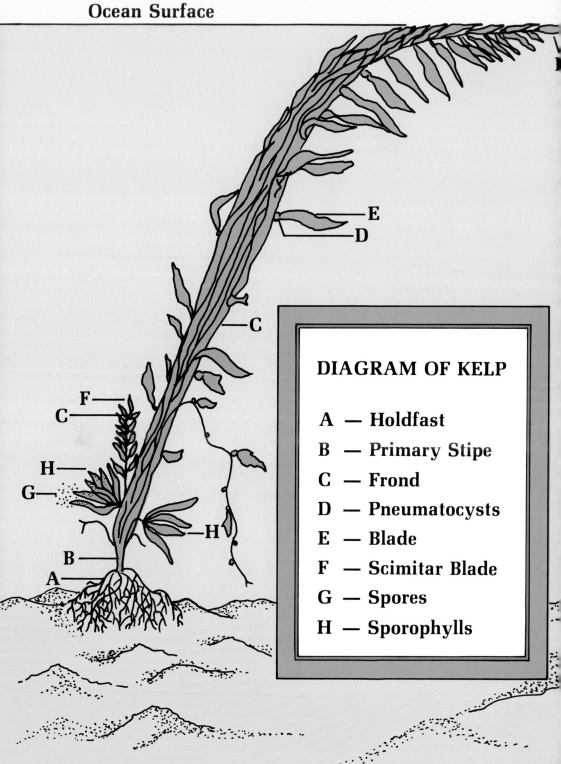

E
D
C
F
C
H
G
H
B
A

DIAGRAM OF KELP

A — Holdfast
B — Primary Stipe
C — Frond
D — Pneumatocysts
E — Blade
F — Scimitar Blade
G — Spores
H — Sporophylls

# 2 The Kelps as Algae

Seaweeds are **algae**, ancient groups of plants that usually live in water. Some algae are as simple as the single cells that sometimes form a green film on the surface of stagnent ponds. Others are as complex as the giant kelps.

Early seaweeds grew in the ocean long before humans ever walked on earth. Algae similar to our present-day green and red seaweeds lived 400 million years ago.

One way to classify, or label, algae is by color. Giant kelp plants are the largest of the brown algae. Like other algae, kelps contain **chlorophyll**, the green coloring matter in plants that absorbs light, making photosynthesis possible. The kelps don't look green because their brown pigment masks the color of chlorophyll.

Algae are different from most plants that grow on land. Algae do not have true roots, true stems, or true leaves. And they do not create seeds to **reproduce**.

Complex Kelp Structure

The lowest part of a giant kelp plant may look like a ball of roots, but it doesn't work in the same way. Roots carry **nutrients**—the substances that living things need to grow and thrive—into the other parts of an ordinary plant. A kelp plant doesn't need roots. The nutrients that it needs are dissolved in seawater, and they are taken in through the surfaces of the whole plant.

What looks like a ball of roots under a kelp plant is called a **holdfast**. A holdfast is a strong tangle of clinging strands that looks like a mound of giant brown spaghetti. It serves to anchor the kelp, usually to a rock on the ocean floor.

Above the holdfast, the part that looks like the main stem of a kelp plant is called the **primary stipe**. A stipe does not contain woody cells. A kelp plant doesn't need anything stiff to hold it up. It needs only to float upright in the water.

Instead of branches, giant kelps grow **fronds**. Long and slender, the fronds look somewhat like vines growing out from the primary stipe. The centers of the fronds are also called **stipes**. As many as 100 fronds can grow above one single holdfast.

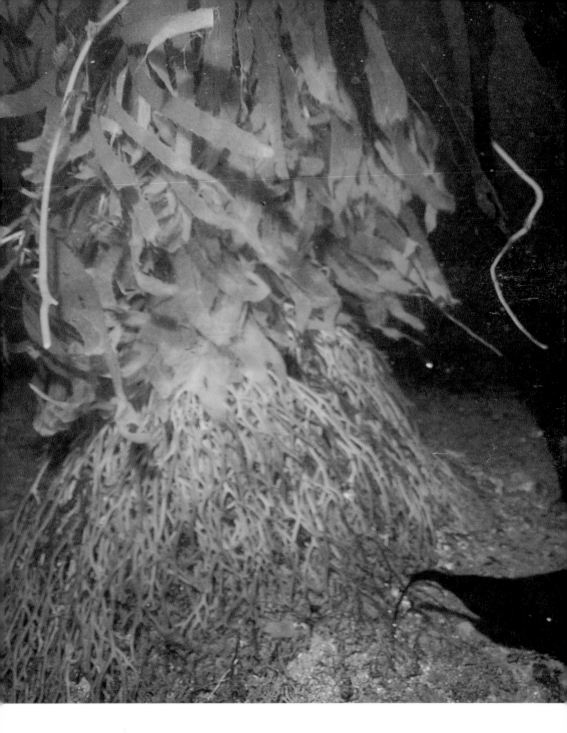

The holdfast of this giant kelp plant serves to anchor it to the ocean floor. The primary stipe and fronds grow above the holdfast. (Richard Rosenthal)

Floats Hold up Kelp

Gas-filled bulbs are spaced along opposite sides of a giant kelp stipe. These bulbs are called **pneumatocysts**. When they are very young, they look like small green peas. They serve as floats holding up the fronds. Since kelp tissues are heavier than water, they would sink without something to hold them up. As the fronds grow bigger, their pneumatocysts enlarge, too. Sometimes the floats are round, sometimes pear-shaped, and sometimes the shape of tiny footballs.

What looks like a leaf on a kelp plant is called a **blade**. Each slim, wavy blade grows out from its own pneumatocyst. The blade is connected to the stipe at a forty-five-degree angle. This form creates the greatest possible space between blades. As a result, they do not shade each other completely from the sunlight that all of them can use in order to grow.

A long frond may have as many as 200 pairs of blades and pneumatocysts along the stipe. When a frond reaches a length of 50 feet (15 meters), it begins to grow very fast—as much as 24 inches (61 centimeters) in 24 hours. When conditions are good, the blades can become nearly 4 feet (1.2 meters) long and 1 foot (30.5 centimeters) wide.

Gas-filled bulbs called pneumatocysts serve as floats holding up the fronds of a giant kelp plant.

At the tip of a frond, where new growth is taking place, a **scimitar blade** unfolds. Named for the curved saber, a type of sword, the scimitar blade is quite wide when it first unfolds. Then it splits from its base to its edge, forming six or more separate blades.

A frond may live for only six months. As older fronds age and die, new ones develop to take their place. When growing conditions are ideal, a giant kelp plant may live for as long as seven years. During that time its separate parts may grow old and die, but new growth replaces them.

Kelp Reproduction

Algae are different from most plants that grow on land in the special way that they reproduce. Instead of creating seeds, as flowering plants do, algae produce **spores**. The spores of giant kelp are small, round, and almost colorless. They appear above the holdfast on clusters of special blades called **sporophylls**. Spores massed close together in their brown cases appear to be patches of brown on the sporophylls. A single adult giant kelp plant can release 70 **trillion** spores per year. Each spore is a single cell with twin "tails," fine hairs moving in waves that carry the spore through the water.

A graceful scimitar blade unfolds at the tip of a giant kelp frond where new growth is taking place. (Steven K. Webster)

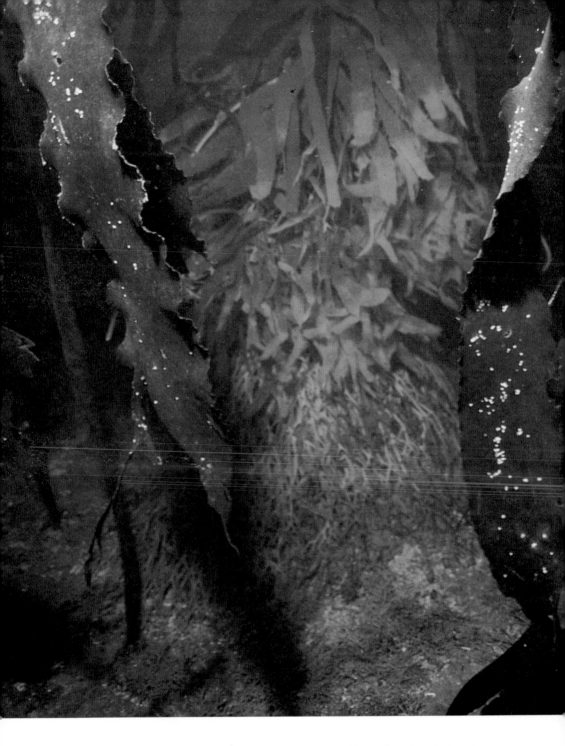

Clusters of sporophylls grow above the holdfast of a giant kelp plant. Spores massed close together in brown cases appear as brown patches on the sporophylls. (Richard Rosenthal)

When these spores start to grow, they do not become new giant kelp plants. Instead, they produce microscopic plants that release male and female sex cells. These sex cells are called **gametes**.

Male gametes also have twin "tails" that move them around in the water in search of female gametes. When male and female gametes combine, they form a **zygote**. The zygote is also microscopic in size. It will start to grow on the ocean floor if there is enough available light. If growing conditions are good, this zygote will become a big spore-bearing plant—another towering giant kelp.

③ Underwater Forests of Giant Kelp

At the surface of the sea a kelp bed may appear to be only a snarl of ugly brown weeds. Underwater, though, it forms a beautiful forest. Giant kelps usually look different in photographs taken underwater because of the way daylight is absorbed by seawater. The light that comes into the ocean, like all natural light, is a mixture of colors. Red, orange, yellow, green, blue, and violet are all part of natural daylight. After sunlight enters seawater, the ocean absorbs, or subtracts, most of the reddish parts of the color in light. Because seawater filters out the red color of natural light, kelp plants can appear to be green in photographs taken underwater. Human vision is not affected in the same way, so the kelp plants look brown to a diver.

Sometimes, however, the color of kelp plants really does change, as if to copy the change of seasons on land. Summer heat makes older parts of kelp plants age faster. The dying parts are yellow or yellow-orange as they break off and settle on the ocean floor.

In this aerial view of kelp beds, the giant kelp plants appear as a mass of brown seaweeds next to a white ship on the blue sea. (Richard Rosenthal)

From underwater, the canopy of a giant kelp bed forms a dense forest. In this photograph the canopy appears close to its true brown color. (Richard Rosenthal)

At other times the kelp forest looks as if it is frosted with snow, but this icing has nothing to do with the weather. Tiny shelled animals sometimes cover kelp plants with patches of white.

A Canopy of Kelp
When kelp fronds have grown as tall as they can, they keep right on growing sideways along the surface

of the sea. As they crowd close to each other, they create the **canopy** of a kelp bed. On land, the upper layer of spreading branches in a crowded forest is also called a canopy.

Under a thick kelp canopy, the underwater forest is deep in shadows. Since other kinds of plants also need sunlight in order to grow, they are seldom found on the sea floor directly beneath a thick kelp canopy. Even the lower parts of the kelp plants do not get enough sunlight to carry on photosynthesis. However, they continue to grow. How is this possible?

Within the stipes of giant kelp plants are microscopic, tubelike channels. Photosynthesis takes place all the time in strong sunlight near the surface. The products of photosynthesis are carried down through these tiny channels in the stipes. This transfer is called **translocation**. Because of translocation, young kelp fronds far below in deep shade receive the energy they need to grow. Without translocation, giant kelps could not form dense underwater forests.

Growing Conditions

Certain conditions in seawater are necessary if giant kelp is to grow well. The water must be cool, within a range of temperatures from about forty-five to seventy-five degrees Fahrenheit (seven to twenty-four degrees Centigrade). Giant kelps grow well near the California coast because there the ocean water is cool. The California Current continues from a stream of cold water that loses heat to the atmosphere as it flows across the northern Pacific Ocean. The chilled water circles south along the western coast of North America, where it provides just the right temperatures for giant kelp.

Sunlight in the water is also necessary. Far below the ocean surface in extremely deep water, kelps would not receive enough light to grow. Off the coast of California, the best depth for giant kelp to grow is in cool water about 30 to 70 feet (9 to 21.5 meters) below the surface. Where the ocean is deeper than 130 feet (39.5 meters), the light is too dim for kelps to grow.

The wave action in the water must be somewhat gentle for giant kelp to thrive. Even though the plants reach an enormous size, they are in danger if the ocean water around them is too rough. They don't usually grow in the zone of the breaking surf. Along the high-energy coastlines of the Pacific Northwest, the force of the waves would tear the big plants to pieces. Species

Giant kelp plants must have sunlight in order to grow. The parts of the kelp nearest the sea's surface receive the most sunlight. (Richard Rosenthal)

such as feather-boa kelp or bull kelp fare better in rough water than giant kelp does because they have different structures that withstand strong wave action with less damage.

Kelps grow best when seawater is clean and clear enough to admit sunlight. If mud or slime oozes onto the ocean floor, it may smother young kelp plants. Shifting sand can be a danger, too.

Food for Giant Kelp

Giant kelp plants need nutrients in water near the surface of the ocean because they absorb their food along all the surfaces of their stipes and blades. However, surface water is usually not as rich in nutrients as deep water. Most marine animals and plants sink to the ocean floor after they die. As their bodies decay, the water around them absorbs the nutrients they once contained.

At times, a natural event comes to the aid of the giant seaweeds. Often in the spring, deep water rich in minerals moves up to the surface. These **upwellings** occur when winds blowing along the coast push surface water away from shore.

When surface water is blown out to sea, deep

water rises from below to take its place. The shape of the sea floor also affects the upwelling of deep water near the coast. This upward motion of deep rich water brings nutrients to the parts of the plants where food is absorbed.

Giant kelp plants get some nutrients in other ways. Rainfall running into the ocean from the land and ocean currents flowing along the surface through the kelp beds both contain minerals. The big seaweeds can absorb and **recycle** some nutrients from within the kelp ecosystem itself. For two to four weeks, if necessary, the plants can live on the minerals stored within their own tissues.

Kelp Territory

In the Southern **Hemisphere**, the giant kelp occurs near every major land mass in the cool-water zones. North of the **equator**, though, it grows only along the western coastline of North America. Why is it found in just one region in the Northern Hemisphere?

Some scientists think that long ago there was a "bridge" of cold water between North and South America. Somehow giant kelp floated north within this unusual river in the sea. Today, the cold-water link between North and South America no longer exists. But while it was there, giant kelp made its way to the north, where it was to become a very important natural resource.

4 A Home in the Sea

In a California underwater forest, a giant kelp plant makes an inviting tree house for a colorful crowd of sea creatures. They are drawn to it by the thousands. Here they spend their lives in a watery maze of secret hiding places, hidden hallways, trap doors, and shifting walls. Here they settle down, eat, rest, hide, and sometimes meet sudden death. Every day the hunters and the hunted play deadly games of hide-and-seek.

A giant kelp plant offers space where encrusting animals can anchor themselves. For every square foot a giant kelp plant covers on the ocean floor, it provides about 14 square feet (1.3 square meters) of surface space above. Scientists call such a ratio a **leaf index**. The leaf index of giant kelp is at least 14. When growing conditions are good, the ratio can be even higher.

Filter Feeders

On a kelp plant there are usually many **sessile** animals—those that attach themselves permanently

In a California underwater forest, giant kelp plants make inviting tree houses for thousands of sea creatures. (Dr. Wheeler North)

to any surface. They are all filter feeders. Sessile animals are usually covered with hard shells to protect themselves from predators. One of the sessile animals is the moss animal. Just a small fraction of an inch long, it lives close to other moss animals in a colony. Each member of the colony builds a little shell around itself. A colony of moss animals forms a lacy network of white lines on the brown kelp.

Hydroids also encrust kelp blades. They attach one end of their strange, hollow-tubed bodies to the kelp. At the other end they have a mouth circled with tiny **tentacles**. When touched, hydroids release small poison-tipped darts to collect food and to keep their enemies from attacking. Another animal has developed a way to avoid the dangerous darts. Without doing any harm to itself, a sea slug can move the hydroid's poison darts through its own body to the ends of its tentacles. In this way it steals the poison darts for its own use.

Kelp detritus from older parts of kelp plants forms an important part of the ocean food chain near the shore. Small bits of kelp tissue attract animals such as the opossum shrimp. These tiny shrimp come into a kelp bed by the thousands to feed on kelp detritus. The shrimp, in turn, attract fish that feed upon them. In a kelp forest, the deadly drama of fish-eat-fish never ends.

Other Inhabitants of the Kelp Tree House

At least 178 different kinds of animals live in the lowest level of the kelp tree house. The kelp gribble chews tunnels in the holdfast. Other empty spaces in the holdfast make a good nursery for a baby fish, sea urchin, or octopus that needs to hide from predators. To escape, small creatures must manage to hide, or move extremely fast, or pretend to be something else. Some kinds of fish change color to blend in with their surroundings.

A fierce moray eel may be hiding in rocks near a kelp holdfast on the ocean floor. Surrounded by "cleaner" shrimp which remove **parasites** from its skin, the moray eel does not always return the favor. A shrimp that goes inside the eel's mouth to clean it may never come out again.

Other animals, such as the California spiny lobster, live near the holdfast. The spiny lobster hardly moves during the day, but at night it prowls around in search of food. Rock scallops and abalone cling to

Fish hide among the holdfasts of kelp plants that were torn loose from the ocean floor and entangled during a storm. (Richard Rosenthal)

California spiny lobsters move about in search of food among the holdfasts of a giant kelp forest. (Charles Arneson)

nearby rocks on the ocean floor. Here, too, are sea urchins that look like purple pincushions with spines poking out in all directions.

Strange, Colorful Fish

Many fish of strange colors and shapes live toward the bottom of the kelp tree house. Not far above the sand, a shovelnose guitarfish glides along. A convictfish wears up-and-down stripes that continue right through its fins. A mottled scorpionfish has spines that release poison when touched. An opaleye floats along, far from the **tidepool** where it began life. Higher in the water a halfmoon swims faster, grazing on kelp for a moment, and then moving on. A skinny pipefish hangs level in the water, looking more like a brown pencil than a fish.

The garibaldi, a brilliant orange fish that grows as long as fifteen inches (thirty-eight centimeters), is the only marine fish in California fully protected by law. The female garibaldi lays bright yellow eggs in a "nest" that the male garibaldi has prepared. It is a cleared-off space on a rock where the male has encouraged short red algae to grow. The algae make the rock a good place for the eggs. The male will then guard the eggs for several weeks as they develop. If threatened, the male garibaldi will attack creatures much larger than himself.

The señorita, a fish that looks like a cigar, often avoids sunlight. It loves the shade of a kelp plant. A señorita sometimes cleans a garibaldi of flealike parasites. At night the señorita burrows into the sand.

Gold-colored kelp snails with gray tops make

The brittle star, a kelp-bed creature, has a habit of breaking off its "arms" when in danger. (Richard Rosenthal)

their way up a kelp plant from the bottom, only to fall off when they reach the end of a blade. They tumble to the ocean floor and start climbing all over again.

The names of many kelp-bed creatures describe them well—sea squirts, bat stars, and brittle stars. Brittle stars have a habit of breaking off "arms" when in danger. The kelpcurler can pull a blade into the shape of a tube and then use it as a place to hide.

A brilliantly colored garibaldi removes a starfish from its carefully guarded nest of red algae on the sea floor. (Richard Rosenthal)

Large carnivores come in search of the big fish that feed near a kelp bed. Pelicans and cormorants drop from the sky, try to snatch a fish, and flap off again. Noisy sea lions and harbor seals make fish disappear in a flash.

Sea Otters

Perhaps the most playful animal in a kelp bed is the sea otter. It dives far underwater for one of its favorite foods—a sea urchin, an abalone, a crab, or a mussel. It may also carry a flat rock back up to the surface. There the otter floats on its back and cradles the rock on its stomach. With its forepaws, the otter smashes its **prey** on the rock until the shellfish breaks open. Then the otter enjoys its snack.

It is hard to believe how much food an active sea otter needs in order to stay alive. Each day of its life, an otter eats an amount of food that weighs one-fourth as much as the otter itself. The cost of feeding just one of the sea otters in the Monterey Bay Aquarium in California is $10,000 per year.

The canopy of a kelp bed is sometimes so thick that shorebirds can stand on it and look for a careless fish or two swimming just below the surface. The

Sea otters feed on creatures in the kelp beds such as these giant red sea urchins, which appear like bristly pincushions on the ocean floor. (Richard Rosenthal)

lanky heron, with its skinny long legs, curlycue neck, and Pinocchio bill, is just as good at fishing from a kelp canopy as from the sandy shore.

Many different forms of life inhabit an underwater kelp forest. Each one uses the forest in its own special way, but all are enriched by the tree house in the ocean. No plant in the sea could make a bigger or a better home than the life-giving giant kelp.

Kelps through the Ages

People have used seaweeds for centuries. In Iceland, an ancient law book refers to claims and permits required to collect marine algae. Early tribes left proof that they feasted upon seaweeds. In China, Sze Teu wrote in 600 B.C.: "Some algae are a delicacy fit for the most honorable guest, even the king himself." People in such countries as China and Japan like to eat seaweeds just because they enjoy their flavor.

A Navigating Tool

Ancient sailors all over the world used kelps to help them navigate in unknown waters. They knew from experience that the sight of large brown seaweeds meant that rocks must be located below.

In 1492 Christopher Columbus ran into strange brown seaweeds after crossing 2,000 miles (3,218 kilometers) of the Atlantic Ocean. He suddenly came upon masses of seaweeds when no land was in sight. Columbus had sailed into the Sargasso Sea, a huge, seaweed-covered area within the Atlantic Ocean. Only the Sargassum plants floating on its surface separate the Sargasso Sea from the open ocean all around it. These unusual seaweeds are not attached to any substrate, and they are not harmed by warm water. Such Sargassum plants may live for hundreds of years. Some marine scientists claim that there are seaweeds floating in the Sargasso Sea today that were there when Columbus sailed into it so long ago.

Another sailor, J.D. Hooker, went on a voyage to explore the Southern Hemisphere in the 1880s. He found old records from the 1500s warning about the coast of South America: "If you see beds of weedes take heed of them and keep off from them." The "weedes" were kelp.

Kelp Trade in Europe

The ashes of kelp made a good fertilizer. In fact, the name *kelp* was an old Gaelic word in the language of the early Highlanders of Scotland. At first, the word referred only to the ashes of the tall brown seaweeds that we now call kelp. During the twelfth and thirteenth centuries, one region on the north coast of France was called "the golden belt." There the crops were far better than those grown inland because farmers along the coast dug seaweeds into their fields. Kelp **tissues** improve farmland by adding minerals to it. They also make the soil easy to break apart, and they help it hold moisture.

Gathering kelp was hard work because the big seaweeds are very heavy when they are wet. In Scotland the men used to collect kelp on the beach. Then the women and children spread out the wet weeds to dry on special low walls built of loose rocks. If the weeds were turned over often as they dried, they were ready to burn after only two days. Women and children burned the dried seaweeds in kilns, round ovens built with rocks on the beach.

Gathering kelp was such messy work that in Ireland the men used to work naked. They burned the kelp on the beach. Then the kelp ashes were boiled to obtain **potash**—the ash left in the pot after boiling. People everywhere used potash when they made soap.

In Great Britain, one kind of kelp was called "sea club." It received this strange name because the men who harvested seaweeds used to fight with each other using kelp stipes instead of clubs.

The ashes of burned kelp were also rich in soda.

This painting by Goya, Two Men Fighting with Clubs, *hangs in the Prado Museum of Madrid, Spain. Kelp stipes, dried until stiff, could be used as "sea clubs."*

Soda ash was used in the process of making glass. When dried kelp was burned in kilns for a long time, it built up a cake of ash that was sometimes about two feet (61 centimeters) thick.

Because kelp ashes were in great demand for fertilizer and for glassmaking, a kelp trade developed in Europe and Great Britain. It was a big business for many years. But then huge deposits of guano—seabird droppings—were found on islands off the coast of Peru in South America. Guano was as deep as 100 feet (30.5 meters) on some of these small islands where seabirds lived. Since guano turned out to be even richer in minerals than seaweed ashes, it soon replaced kelp as a good source of fertilizer. And when glassmakers found other sources of soda ash, the demand for kelp seemed to be at an end.

However, French kelp burners had paved the way for an important new discovery. In 1811, a French chemist noticed violet-colored crystals in the ashes of burned kelp. He had discovered iodine.

Iodine Found in Kelp

Iodine is an important substance. In very small amounts, it is necessary to control growth in the human body. For centuries people had known that eating seaweeds or fish would prevent goiter, an enlargement of the thyroid gland. People who get enough iodine in their food do not develop this condition. Iodine dissolved in alcohol is an **antiseptic**. Certain infections, including ringworm and sore throat, respond to treatment with iodine.

The discovery of iodine revived the kelp trade for a

time. In Scotland factories seemed to spring up almost overnight to obtain iodine from kelp. But before long other ways to produce iodine were found.

Kelp Harvesting in the New World

A new interest in big brown seaweeds shifted the next round of kelp harvesting to the New World. The events that would lead to World War I were beginning to brew in Europe. Potash, used to make explosives, could no longer be obtained from Germany, the best source at that time. Long before war broke out in Europe, it was clear that the United States needed a new place to find potash if it wanted to prepare for war.

Giant kelp was an ideal source of potash. Huge kelp beds grew along the west coasts of both North and South America. Because of the First World War, a new kelp-collecting industry was born.

Workers cut the big seaweeds by hand and pulled them, dripping wet, onto barges. Next the kelp was delivered to factories, where it was treated to recover both potash and acetone, another substance used to make explosives. In the United States, the makers of gunpowder and bombs no longer had to depend on other countries for their raw materials. Business was booming for the kelp collectors until the war was over.

The war's end did not cause the end of the kelp-collecting industry. Something else was discovered in kelp, a substance that occurs nowhere else—algin. And in the years to come, algin would become so important that the demand for kelp would be stronger than ever.

6 Kelps, the Source of Algin

Algin will probably turn out to be the most valuable substance ever found in kelp. It is part of the **cell walls** of the monster seaweeds. Algin makes the surface of the kelp plants slippery, and it allows them to bend and stretch as the ocean water moves.

Algin was discovered many years before it was ever put to use. Back in the 1880s, an English chemist, E.C. Stanford, set out to find a new use for kelp. He wanted to discover a new reason for harvesting the huge brown seaweeds because the kelp trade in Great Britain was dying.

A Sticky Substance

In 1883, Stanford was proud to announce that while he was working with kelp tissues, he had found "a unique substance of remarkable properties. . .to which I have given the name algin." When Stanford made his report to the public, no one paid any attention. For more than forty years, algin was thought of only as a strange scientific curiosity. No one could imagine at that time that algin would ever be worth anything.

Years later, in the 1920s, research scientists began to take a fresh look at the gummy part of kelp tissues that Stanford had named algin. They found that algin could do some very special things. It could be used to control the flow of fluids in surprising ways.

Within a few years, people began to harvest kelp just to obtain its algin. In 1929, a new company was founded in San Diego, California, to process kelp. The name of the company was Kelco, and today Kelco manufactures more algin products than any other company in the world. Many kinds of kelp are harvested in countries from South America to northern Europe to South Africa, China, Korea, and Japan. Some of the kelp is used as food, and some is processed to manufacture algin products.

The Salts of Algin

The algin taken from giant kelp is treated to make many different products, including **alginates**. These are salts of algin that dissolve easily in water.

Alginates are used in many different kinds of

Loaded with giant kelp, a Kelco harvesting ship cuts through a kelp bed near San Diego, California.

manufacturing. One early process made use of the way alginates dissolve in water. First the alginates were spun into an artificial silk thread. This fiber could be woven with others into a special type of cloth. Then, because the threads made with alginates could be dissolved, the cloth was treated so that these threads would vanish. The other threads did not change. This "disappearing fiber" method of weaving was used to make unusual new kinds of cloth.

Alginates can be used to form a film that helps spread the shiny coating onto high-grade cardboard. Some types of paper with a shiny surface are made with alginates. **Gels** are formed with alginates, too. A dental gel, more solid than liquid, helps a dentist make a model of a tooth.

Alginates also keep salad dressings mixed together. Whenever oil and water are mixed together, they make a liquid that would normally divide into layers. By forming a very thin coating around each little droplet of the mixture, alginates keep mixtures of oil, water, and vinegar smooth.

Alginates are used in many kinds of food. They are in the glaze that makes some doughnuts shiny, and they improve the texture of frostings on other bakery goods. Alginates keep the head of foam on a glass of beer frothy for a long time. They make fruit drinks smooth. Because they form thick solutions, they make milkshakes creamy. Alginates keep some types of whipped cream smooth, and they are used to thicken pancake syrup.

Every day of our lives, most of us use products that are made with some form of algin. Cottage cheese

Alginates are used in many kinds of food, including the desserts shown in this picture.

and catsup contain alginates. So do medicines and cosmetics. Alginates are used to make babies' rubber pants, automobile tires, glazed tiles, and charcoal briquets. Even commercial lion food contains an alginate.

Processing Algin Products

After kelp tissues are harvested, their algin breaks down quickly. For this reason, giant kelp plants are not left standing for long after being cut. After they are brought ashore, they are drawn into the factory through an auger device. The kelp pieces are pushed along through a giant screw turning inside a huge tube, in much the same way that food is forced through a meat grinder or snow is hurled through a snow blower.

Inside the factory, the chopped kelp is washed and cooked before its algin is removed. The algin is then treated with chemicals, filtered, and finally milled into powders to fill the needs of buyers who want alginates for many special purposes.

A market exists even for the leftover parts of kelp tissues that are filtered out when alginates are made. These are the fibers of the cell walls left behind when the algin is taken out of kelp. This leftover material is sold as a soil conditioner for growing plants.

Kelp-harvesting companies help support the efforts to protect the kelp beds. In California, for example, Kelco maintains a Marine Resource Department. Along with scientists from the Scripps Institution of Oceanography, The California Institute of Technology, and the California Department of Fish and Game, the company works to keep the kelp beds as healthy as possible.

Constant Demand for Kelp

The scientist who first named the sticky material in kelp tissues must have been disappointed when his discovery of algin did not save the kelp trade in Scotland. Today, more than a century after Mr. Stanford announced his news, the future of kelp harvesting is no longer in doubt. Because of the market for algin, kelp is always in demand. There are buyers for all the algin products made, and the only place in the world to find algin is in the brown seaweeds called kelp.

A Trip on a Kelp Harvester

A kelp-harvesting ship is actually a seagoing lawn mower. It cuts only the canopy of a kelp bed. The crew of a big harvester can bring aboard a full load of kelp—as much as 500 tons (454 metric tons)—in one day.

The captain and his crew of five spend long hours on the job. In the summer, their work starts at 4:30 or 5 A.M. when the harvester leaves the dock, and in the winter, one hour later. Kelp harvesting is an all-day job and a year-round business.

Leaving the Dock

Before the captain and his crew begin their work, the chief **marine biologist** of a harvesting company goes up in an airplane to look over the kelp beds. After a thick canopy has been located, the harvesting company orders one of its ships to get ready to leave.

The two main engines start with the rattle and clatter that is normal for diesel engines. The captain

A kelp harvesting ship has an open container, or kelp bin, on the deck in the middle of the ship. The bin holds the cut kelp sent up to it from conveyor belts that are lowered into the water for kelp harvesting.

gives one long blast on the whistle to let everybody know that the kelp harvester is leaving the dock. After the ship is under way, the crew has time to eat a hot meal. Later in the day, when the workers are busy harvesting, they will have time only for snacks.

When the harvester reaches the kelp bed, the captain looks around to make sure that no sea otters are taking a nap in the canopy. Sometimes otters wrap strands of kelp around their bodies to keep from drifting away from the kelp bed while they sleep. Although they are totally relaxed as they float on their backs, otters would seldom be able to sleep through the noisy approach of a kelp harvester. To make sure of their safety, however, the captain blows his whistle and slows down.

The Cutting Process

When it is time to start harvesting, the engineer and his helper leave the engine room and go to the deck at the **stern**. Two **conveyor belts**, known as "**drapers**," are lowered into the water. Cutting blades are located under the lower edges of the drapers. The knives will be set at a level four feet (1.2 meters) below the surface. Then the drapers are "dogged down," or locked into position.

A kelp harvester backs into a kelp bed. An extra propeller and rudder on the **bow** of the ship are used to move it into the kelp. The captain has a very good view of the kelp cutters. The **wheelhouse** where he oversees the whole cutting process is located thirty feet (nine meters) above the knives.

If the wind is blowing, as it often does on the

ocean, the harvester will drift sideways as the captain heads it into the kelp bed. When this happens, the captain steers into the wind at an angle in order to go straight.

The drapers rattle and screech when the knives first start to cut kelp. As the harvester moves along, the seaweed cuttings flop onto the drapers and start their trip upward. To keep the slippery kelp from falling off, spikes stick out of both conveyor belts. The spikes are about six inches (fifteen centimeters) high and as big around as a person's finger. After the kelp reaches the top of the drapers, it drops down into the kelp bin—an open container on the deck in the middle of the ship.

If all the kelp stayed right where it landed, that end of the kelp bin would soon be filled to overflowing, and the other end would be empty. The heavy cuttings must be spread out evenly in the kelp bin. To spread them out, a "loading fork" is dropped onto the kelp cuttings when the pile reaches a height of five feet (1.5 meters). The fork is used to drag some of the seaweed cuttings to the far end of the kelp bin. It looks like a giant rake and weighs about 200 pounds (91 kilograms).

To the right of this picture, a giant "loading fork" drags freshly cut giant kelp to the far end of the harvesting ship's kelp bin.

A great deal of water comes aboard with the kelp cuttings. Little by little, it will drain off and run back into the sea.

The harvester does not start at the edge of a kelp bed. The first path it cuts is straight through the middle of the canopy. The captain takes the harvester through the center of the kelp bed, and then he makes a turn in open water to come back. The next path he cuts will be close beside the first one. The harvesting pattern gets wider and wider as the day goes on.

Although the workers are tired when they finish harvesting, they must also work at night. Each crew member stays on duty for four hours of watch, followed by four hours of sleep. Each has a bunk in the bow of the ship, while the captain has separate quarters.

After the Harvest

After the kelp canopy is harvested, the lower parts of the plants, and the sea floor under them, will receive more sunlight. More light will encourage a new spurt of growth. On land, the same thing happens when the upper layer of a thick hedge is cut off—new leaves begin to grow as soon as sunlight reaches the lower parts of the plants. When sunlight reaches the sea floor again, new kelp plants can begin to grow as soon as gametes are released to unite and form zygotes.

The captain says that the hardest part of his job is trying to guess what the weather is going to do when he is coming home with a full load of kelp. If a sudden storm should come up, he might have to head for shelter out of the wind near an island. Although storms do not come as a surprise very often, the men have learned from experience to take extra food along just in case bad weather should delay their return.

When the kelp harvester comes back to port, its load of seaweed is placed in another kelp bin on the same dock where the trip began. Right after the ship is unloaded, it smells strongly of seaweed. The harvester's kelp bin is washed clean after every trip. If another canopy is thick enough to be cut, the harvester may turn right around and head back out to sea.

The demand for algin products never stops. The growth of giant kelp never stops, either, if conditions are good. Even a kelp bed that has just had a haircut will normally start to grow another canopy right away. Within a few short months it will be ready to harvest again. A bed of giant kelp is an outstanding natural resource that renews itself again and again.

The Mystery of the Disappearing Kelp

Kelp forests grow better in some years than in others. The temperature of the water and the supply of nutrients can change from year to year. In southern California, however, something very puzzling began to happen to the kelp beds in the early 1940s. The bad years were never followed by good years. The kelp beds were in trouble, and nobody knew why.

What was happening? And what could be done? A team of scientific detectives went to work to solve the mystery. Dr. Wheeler North, already an expert in scuba (Self-Contained Underwater Breathing Apparatus) diving, was chosen to lead a study of the kelp forests.

The First Suspect

Polluted water was the first suspect. San Diego and Los Angeles were dumping more and more treated sewage into the ocean with each passing year. Kelp plants near sewer **outfalls** had been the first to die.

Was sewage killing the kelp forests? Many people

Dr. Wheeler North, dressed in scuba diving gear, prepares to make a dive along the coast of southern California.

thought so. Dr. North and other scientists, also scuba divers, started to look for clues. They dived into murky water near sewer outfalls at thirty- to fifty-foot (nine- to fifteen-meter) depths, usually good places for kelp to grow. The sludge oozing from sewer outfalls could bury young plants. But what about other plants nearby? Had polluted water killed them?

Some scientists began to experiment in laboratories. Their plan was to mix sewage with seawater to see if kelp plants could grow in it. What happened was a surprise. The kelps did very well. In fact, kelp photosynthesis was 50 percent higher in this polluted water than it was under normal conditions. Clearly, the sewage contained nutrients that kelp plants were using.

Sewage contains nitrogen, and nitrogen is one of the substances that plants need in order to grow. The scientists were observing that kelp plants do not seem to know the difference between nitrogen in sewage and nitrogen in rainfall runoff from land. The damage to kelp plants would come from not receiving any nitrogen at all.

Dr. North and his expert detectives were no closer to solving the mystery than they had been in the beginning. Whatever was killing the kelp was still at large.

Looking for Other Clues

The scientists looked for other clues. They went to sea in a tiny boat during storms to measure the force of the waves sweeping through the kelp beds. They watched huge rocks shift position on the ocean floor as they swam among elephant seals and killer whales. They traveled from Mexico to central California looking for the basic information needed to help save the dying kelp.

At last they caught one type of killer in the act. The scientists surprised even themselves with their discovery. Small sea urchins, innocent-looking, bristly pincushions that live on the ocean floor, were killing kelp plants.

When the balance of nature is the way it should be in the kelp beds, sea urchins are not a problem. But when there are no predators to remove sea urchins, they multiply too fast. So many of them are hunting for food that none of them can find enough to eat. Then, like clouds of locusts on land, they destroy everything in their path. They leave nothing behind. If the primary stipe of a magnificent giant kelp happens to be in their way, they simply chew across it. The whole plant is set adrift. It floats away, and so does the home and

Sea urchins, hunting for food, attack the holdfast and primary stipe of a giant kelp plant. (Steven K. Webster)

shelter and food supply of all the creatures that depend on the kelp.

Dr. David Leighton once observed an army of urchins moving thirty feet (nine meters) a month across the ocean floor, leaving only bare rocks behind. "Starving urchins will eat anything," says Dr. North. "I've even seen them chewing the wax off sunken milk cartons."

Sea Urchins and Sea Otters

Why had sea urchins taken over the waters of southern California? The answer to that question goes back to the last century. Sadly, people were at fault. Human beings had upset the balance of nature in the ocean. They nearly wiped out a whole population of the most powerful predators that control sea urchins—the sea otters.

Otters are furry **mammals** that used to thrive in kelp forests from Mexico to Alaska. Sea otters live on the shellfish that they find in the kelp beds. Sea otters prey upon sea urchins. Although other creatures prey upon sea urchins—lobsters and fish, for example—only the sea otters prevent sea urchins from taking over an entire area. Unfortunately for the otters, their

When sea otters prey upon sea urchins, they leave "otter middens" such as the remains of sea urchins shown here. (Richard Rosenthal)

beautiful brown fur became a high-fashion item. Fur traders killed so many otters for their pelts that they no longer had any effect on the kelp ecosystem. As a result, sea urchins took over the territory.

Dr. North was sure of the link among otters and sea urchins and kelp beds when he found out that a thick kelp bed had come back to life in Monterey Bay. Before, in the same area, Dr. North had observed only a few scattered kelp plants surviving among acres and acres of sea urchins on the ocean floor.

What had happened? Sea otters, once in danger of dying out in Monterey Bay, had come under the care of a group of people called "The Friends of the Sea Otter." More and more otters were eating enough sea urchins to bring them again into balance with other animals and plants in the region. The otters had rescued the kelp from the urchins.

But what could save the southern California kelp beds? Sea otters no longer lived there.

Dr. North admits that he wanted to try to bring some of the Monterey Bay sea otters to southern California. But otters, twirling all the time to create air bubbles under their fur, might tangle and drown in any net used to capture them. Nobody wanted to take that risk. "Besides," says Dr. North, "even if we brought otters to southern California, we couldn't ever be sure that they would stay. They might turn right around and swim back up to Monterey."

Controlling the Sea Urchins

It was clear that the scientists themselves would have to take over the part that otters play in the kelp

For many years sea otters helped maintain the natural balance of sea creatures in the giant kelp beds. Now, in some areas, few are left to prey upon sea urchins. (Charles Arneson)

ecosystem. They would have to be the ones to kill sea urchins. It came down to a choice between two forms of marine life. The kelp beds were in danger of dying out. The sea urchins were not.

A research team removed all urchins from one area to see what would happen. They had to use quick-lime, a substance used to clear oyster beds of predators. "Within two months," says Dr. North, "we had a healthy little kelp patch." Without sea urchins on the scene, young kelp plants had a chance to grow.

When the kelp ecosystem is in balance, sea urchins stay in the **crevices** where they usually live. There they get all the food they need from kelp detritus that naturally settles down on them. They don't multiply into starving armies that destroy everything in their path.

A new business has started that is helping to keep sea urchins from multiplying too fast in the kelp beds. The sea urchins are now being harvested for their eggs. These are considered a delicious food by people in Japan and in many other countries. The harvesting of sea urchins helps maintain a healthy balance in the kelp ecosystem.

Scientists who want to protect kelp beds watch the ocean to see that seawater stays clean and clear enough to admit sunlight. People must become aware that they cannot use the ocean as a garbage dump. Giant kelp began to grow again near Palos Verdes when toxic chemicals, including DDT, were no longer discharged into the sea there. If we protect our kelp forests, we also keep the ocean safe for other forms of marine life. In the end, the quality of life in the oceans will have an influence on the quality of human life.

How the Weather Affects the Kelps

The oceans of the world have their own weather and their own disasters. In the areas of the Pacific Ocean where the giant kelp lives, normal weather patterns aid its growth. Giant kelp grows where the ocean water is cool and the wave action mild.

The cold ocean currents are powerful unseen rivers that flow within the sea. They are set in motion by the winds above them. The weather in the sea and the weather in the earth's atmosphere are closely linked. Whenever the winds change, the ocean currents beneath them change, too.

The World's Weather Machine

The "engine" of the world's weather machine is run by the heat at the equator. There the warmest air on earth rises straight up into the atmosphere. As long as this weather machine runs in its normal way, kelp plants are safe in cool water. If the weather patterns change, though, they can suffer terrible damage.

Such a change seems to happen about every three to seven years. The trouble is called "El Niño," the Spanish word for the Christ-child, because El Niño often begins around the Christmas season. It was named by the fishermen of Ecuador and Peru, in South America. Their fortunes depend on the cold Humboldt Current, also called the Peru Current, that flows northward along their coastline. These fishermen haul in huge catches of fish in a normal year. In fact, they take in one-fifth of the total fish caught in the whole world. Their fishing grounds are rich in nutrients brought up from the depths of the sea by the Humboldt Current.

But El Niño can suddenly turn these good fishing grounds into a stinking mass of rotting plankton and dead fish. Why does this happen? The Humboldt Current disappears. It is blocked by warm water that El Niño causes to back up from the equator, instead of flowing west as it usually does.

Winds and Currents
When the world's weather machine is running as usual, water at the equator is pushed westward by winds that are steady and strong. These winds are called **trade winds**, and they are constant. They

When a storm pounds the California coast, giant kelp beds can suffer terrible damage.

normally blow toward the equator, where warm air is rising constantly. Because of the rotation of the earth, the trade winds blow toward the west. They drive warm surface water ahead of them, pushing it away from the kelp beds along the American coastlines. The trade winds are so strong that they set up powerful currents at the equator, carrying warm water all the way across the Pacific Ocean. So much warm water is pushed to the west that it builds up in a layer several feet high near the Philippine Islands.

When these great currents at the equator bump into the land masses of Asia, they turn aside. In the Northern Hemisphere, the current turning north from the equator is still warm as it flows past Japan. Then it continues in a great circle across the cold northern part of the Pacific, where the water loses heat to the arctic atmosphere. By the time the current gets to North America, it is well chilled. It is called the California Current as it sweeps along the west coast. Its cool temperature is ideal for the giant kelp beds.

The same pattern occurs in the Southern Hemisphere. Warm water flowing west at the equator is turned aside before it gets to Australia. It circles back across the colder parts of the southern ocean, losing

This map shows the pattern of currents in the Pacific Ocean.

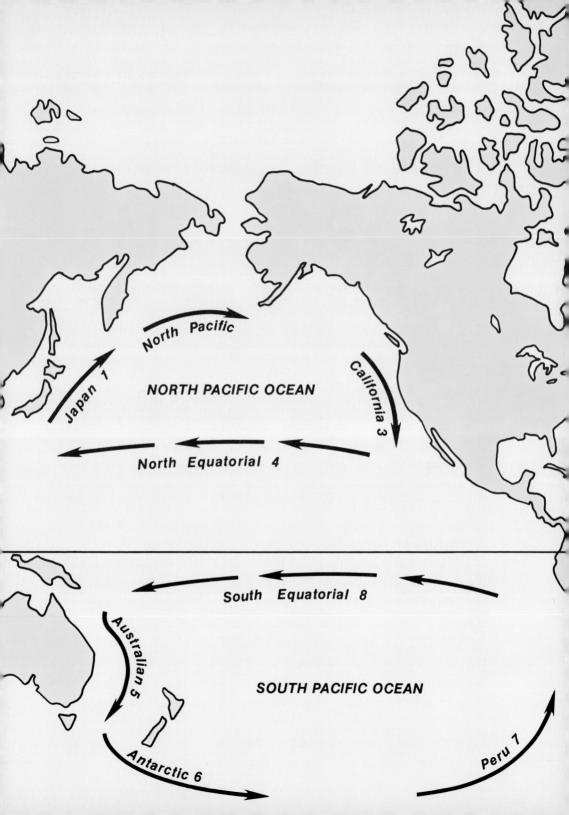

heat to the polar atmosphere of Antarctica. When the current flows toward South America again, it becomes the Humboldt, or Peru Current, and it is cold. The cold water is ideal for the kelp beds along the coast, and it lifts nutrients from the bottom of the sea to enrich the fishing grounds of Peru.

The Arrival of El Niño

When El Niño arrives, however, all the normal patterns change. The trade winds quit blowing. **Equatorial** waters stop moving west. Because the ocean currents are not flowing in their normal way, warm water floods back toward Peru and causes the atmosphere there to become warmer than usual. Violent storms develop. Kelp beds can be dashed to pieces when these fierce storms churn up the ocean.

The last El Niño, in 1983, was the strongest on record. It caused terrible weather all over the world, but the most dramatic changes were in the Pacific Ocean. Surface temperatures were far above normal in many places. Strange things happened.

On Christmas Island near the equator, 17 million seabirds suddenly disappeared from their ancient nesting grounds, leaving their young to die. The level of the

A giant kelp plant floats free among other kelp plants after being torn loose by a winter storm along the Pacific coast. (Richard Rosenthal)

sea was eight inches (twenty centimeters) above normal in San Diego, California. In Monterey Bay, fishermen were surprised to pull in barracuda and tuna. Sea horses and marlin appeared as far north as San Francisco, hundreds of miles from their usual habitat. Salmon that normally run in waters near Oregon and Washington had to swim to Alaska to reach cold water. Giant kelp plants had no way to escape El

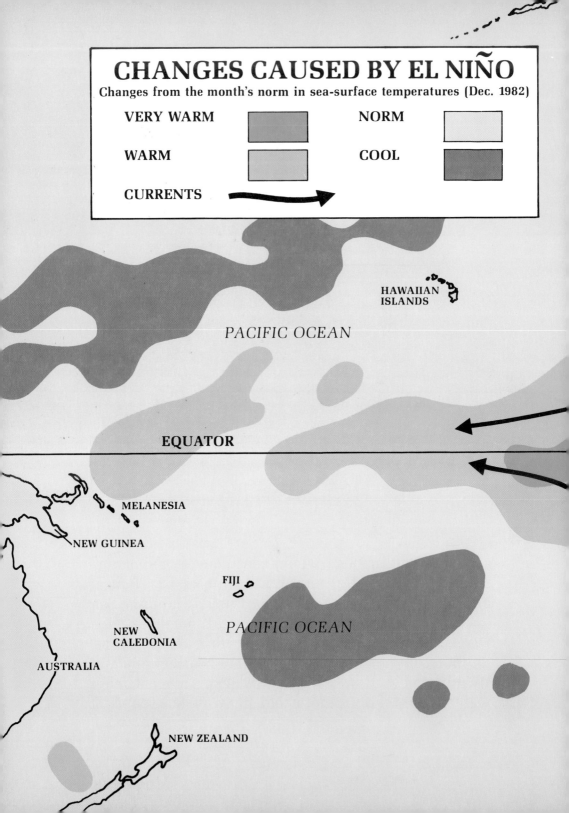

CHANGES CAUSED BY EL NIÑO

Changes from the month's norm in sea-surface temperatures (Dec. 1982)

VERY WARM   NORM

WARM   COOL

CURRENTS

HAWAIIAN
ISLANDS

PACIFIC OCEAN

EQUATOR

MELANESIA

NEW GUINEA

FIJI

NEW
CALEDONIA

PACIFIC OCEAN

AUSTRALIA

NEW ZEALAND

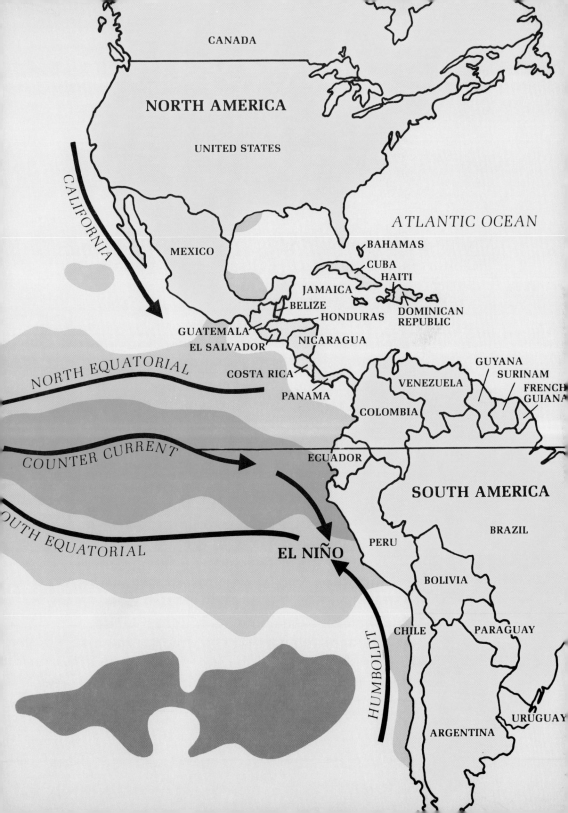

Niño. A thick canopy of giant kelp near Palos Verdes, California, was 90 percent destroyed by the storms of 1983.

El Niño caused the weather to play a game of hopscotch all over the world. Regions that normally get almost no rainfall were flooded with twelve feet (about four meters) of rain. Other places, usually drenched with rain, suddenly got none. The cold, rainy winters of some regions were unusually mild. The world's weather machine went haywire and even weather scientists couldn't explain why.

Tracking El Niño

Scientists from all over the world came together to discuss the weird weather. They could not agree on what caused El Niño. Some thought that the flip-flops of weather had made the trade winds die down. Others blamed El Chichón, a Mexican volcano that belched dust into the atmosphere a year earlier. They believed that this dust had blocked enough sunlight to disturb the weather. Others thought that perhaps some unusual storms on the surface of the sun caused El Niño.

Even though weather experts could not agree on the causes of the El Niño of 1983, they made plans to keep track of it in the future. The Jet Propulsion Laboratory in Pasadena, California, made plans to launch a special **satellite** in 1990. Called TOPEX, for **Topographical** Explorer, it will measure the height of the sea in relation to the center of the earth. TOPEX will keep track of where Pacific Ocean waters are moving.

No matter how often El Niño may return or how much damage it may do, no one believes that the biggest of the brown seaweeds will ever be completely destroyed. Kelp experts know how to grow giant kelp plants in laboratories. In fact, they have transplanted, or moved, them into the sea with some success. Scientists may be able to make sure that the great monster kelps will never vanish from the face of the earth.

Kelp Farms of the Future

The population of the earth is nearly 5 billion people. According to some forecasts, we may have more than twice that many people by the year 2010. As it is, two-thirds of us go to sleep poorly fed, or hungry, every single night. In less than twenty-five years, how will we ever be able to feed twice as many people as we already have on earth?

Dr. Howard A. Wilcox of the U.S. Navy Ocean Systems Center in San Diego, California, believes that we will have to turn to the sea if we are to raise enough food for everyone on earth in the future. The actual design of an ocean farm system has been under study for years.

Kelp Crops

If plant crops are to grow anywhere, they must receive the energy of sunlight in order to carry on photosynthesis. Abundant solar energy exists on the surface of the world, but not enough

Dr. Howard Wilcox has designed a system for a huge ocean farm that could produce kelp for human use in the future.

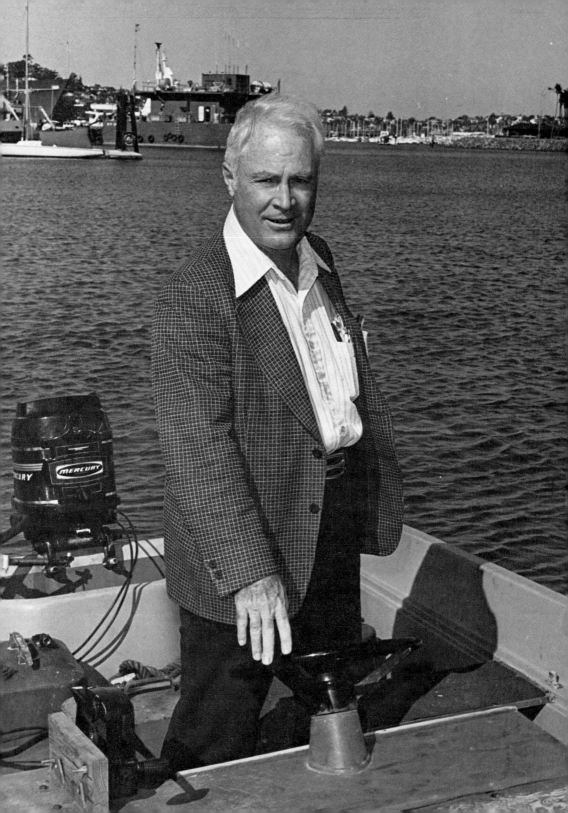

good farmland. Before long we will need more than twice as much food as we raise today. We don't have twice as much farmland to use.

We do have 10,000 times more solar energy on earth than all other forms of energy combined. If we are to make use of this free energy, we will have to go to the surface of the sea. Our oceans cover about 70 percent of the earth's surface.

Giant kelp is the ideal crop to grow in ocean farms. These monster seaweeds grow so fast that we could grow an enormous amount of food if we raised kelp in ocean farms. Unfortunately, most of us in the Western world don't like the taste of kelp. People in other parts of the world, though, have enjoyed seaweeds as sea vegetables for centuries.

In Asia kelp farming in the ocean is already a big business. The People's Republic of China harvests more than two million wet tons of kelp per year. That is more than three times the amount harvested in Japan and about five times the amount in the Republic of Korea. China has developed species of kelp that grow well in warm water, increasing the country's total crop by one-third. Half of China's kelp is used as food. Many southern Asian countries must rely on

The oceans of the world have abundant solar energy that could be used to grow "crops" of kelp and other seaweeds.

imports to satisfy the demand for seaweed foods.

Although plenty of solar energy exists at the surface of the open ocean, this water layer does not have a good supply of nutrients. Surface waters of the seas are often "**biological deserts,**" poor in nutrients that growing plants require. Some type of pumping system would be necessary to supply giant kelp plants with deep water rich in nutrients.

Sea Farm Plans

The best sea farm, Dr. Wilcox believes, would be an enormous structure that floats on ocean currents. In the Pacific Ocean, a kelp farm would drift slowly in an enormous circle, moving clockwise in the Northern Hemisphere. The direction of the farm's drifting could be controlled as it floated slowly toward islands in the sea. Diesel engines inside huge buoys at the edges of the farm would supply the power to control its position in the current.

The plan that Dr. Wilcox has designed would create an ocean farm of 100,000 acres (40,000 hectares). The plants would grow on strong plastic lines stretched from 100 feet (30.5 meters) below the surface of the sea. Kelp experts have already proved that holdfasts can

A U.S. Navy diver attaches a giant kelp plant to a plastic line stretched beneath the ocean surface in an experimental kelp sea farm.

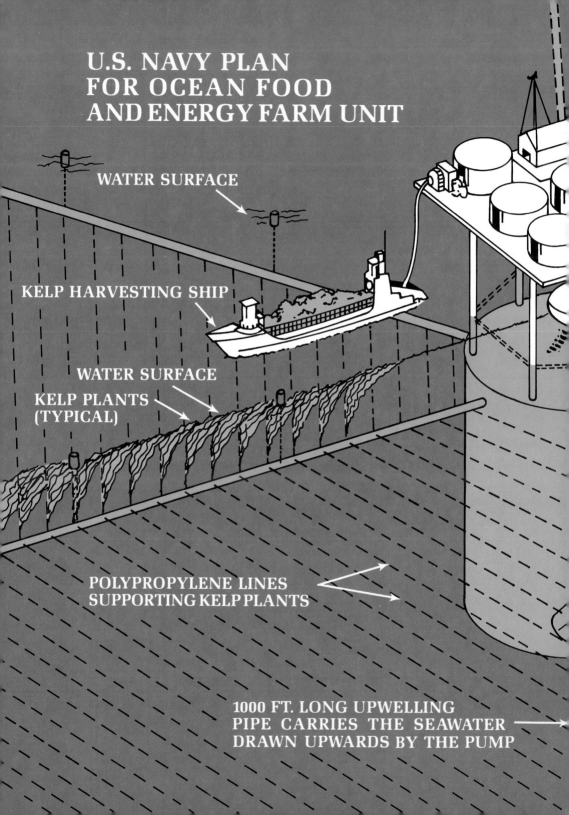

U.S. NAVY PLAN
FOR OCEAN FOOD
AND ENERGY FARM UNIT

WATER SURFACE

KELP HARVESTING SHIP

WATER SURFACE

KELP PLANTS
(TYPICAL)

POLYPROPYLENE LINES
SUPPORTING KELP PLANTS

1000 FT. LONG UPWELLING
PIPE CARRIES THE SEAWATER
DRAWN UPWARDS BY THE PUMP

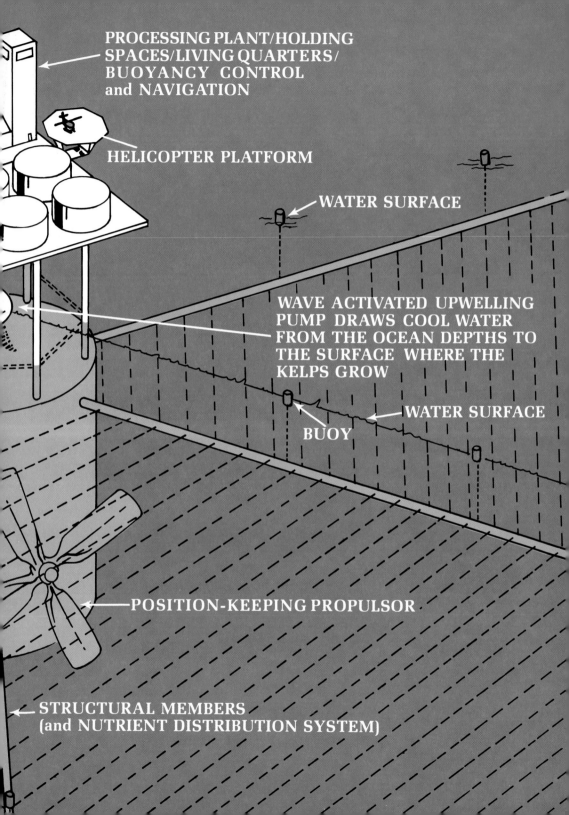

PROCESSING PLANT/HOLDING
SPACES/LIVING QUARTERS/
BUOYANCY CONTROL
and NAVIGATION

HELICOPTER PLATFORM

WATER SURFACE

WAVE ACTIVATED UPWELLING
PUMP DRAWS COOL WATER
FROM THE OCEAN DEPTHS TO
THE SURFACE WHERE THE
KELPS GROW

WATER SURFACE

BUOY

POSITION-KEEPING PROPULSOR

STRUCTURAL MEMBERS
(and NUTRIENT DISTRIBUTION SYSTEM)

anchor the plants to these lines as well as they do to rocks on the ocean floor. The lines in an ocean farm would be attached to structures that would cover a huge area of ocean surface—ten to twelve miles (sixteen to nineteen kilometers) in **diameter**. The skeleton of the farm would look like the ribs of a gigantic umbrella spread upside-down underwater.

One of Dr. Wilcox's ocean farms would float westward from California on the current at the equator. When the farm floated close to Japan, the current would carry it north. After it drifted into the northern Pacific Ocean on the Japan Current, it would travel through icy polar water. In time it would float into the cold California Current flowing south. The ocean farm would drift so slowly on the currents that from a passing ship it would not appear to be moving at all.

But what about the high temperature of the water along the equator? Wouldn't it kill the kelp plants?

No, answers Dr. Wilcox, because a pumping system would bring up a constant supply of cold water from the depths of the ocean. Coming from 1,000 feet (305 meters) below the surface, this water would be cool enough for giant kelp plants to survive. The power of the ocean waves would be used to provide an upwelling of deep water. A float would rise and fall with the passing waves. The float would operate a **lift pump**. Kelp plants in the ocean farm would be flooded with so much cold water that they would stay healthy, even in the tropics.

To be successful, a big farm would take careful planning. The position of such a big structure in the ocean would have to be shown on charts of shipping lanes. Many countries would have to work together to create laws that would protect these farms in the sea.

Questions Remain

Many questions remain to be answered. What would happen if the cooled ocean farm changed the weather above it? What if the presence of such a big structure altered the currents in the sea? Would a floating kelp farm be likely to use up all the nutrients in the deep water underneath it?

The idea of an ocean farm raises difficult questions. However, scientists have already gone beyond the first stages of experimenting with ocean farms. They already know that giant kelp plants will grow when their holdfasts are attached to nothing more than plastic lines. They have proved that kelp plants will grow well in rich water pumped to the surface from the depths of the sea. They know that kelp spores will combine to create zygotes that will start to grow on plastic lines. As a result, they are sure that kelp plants in a sea farm will be able to reproduce themselves.

Scientists sometimes raise as many questions as they answer. Yet in the future our world will face serious problems. Will the world's people be wise enough to solve them?

Giant kelp, and kelp farms that float in the sea, may help us meet the challenges to come. If we care about the future of the giant kelp, and we think about the future of our planet Earth, then we can all be thankful that these magnificent monster seaweeds exist.

# Appendix A:
Learning More
About Giant Kelp

The following activities will help you learn more about giant kelp. Choose one or more to begin working on today.

1. If possible, plan a trip to the Monterey Bay Aquarium, 886 Cannery Row, Monterey, California. Take a notebook with you. Draw a diagram of a giant kelp plant and label the parts. Also sketch the fish and sea otters that you see. Label them with the scientific names that you find on the signs.

2. Visit a beach near a bed of giant kelp. If you see some kelp washed up on the sand, stomp on the pneumatocysts. What sound do you hear? How long do you think the kelp has been on the beach? How does it smell? How many different kinds of marine creatures can you count on the kelp?

3. In a grocery store, look for items that contain some kind of alginate. Check the labels for the lists of ingredients. (See Chapter 6 of this book for suggestions of products that might contain alginates. Sodium alginate is a common one.) How many different kinds of alginates can you find?

4. Weigh yourself. Divide the number of pounds you weigh by four. Then go to your kitchen and set out cans and packages of food until you have a total of as many pounds as your weight divided by four. Can you imagine eating that much food in one day by yourself? Aren't you glad you're not a sea otter?

Appendix B:
Scientific Names
for Sea Animals

Sea creatures, like all living things, have two kinds of names. The first is their *common name*, a name in the everyday language of an area where they are found. An animal often has a number of different common names in different languages. Also, several different animals may be known by the same common name.

The second kind of name is their *scientific name*. This is a Latin name assigned by scientists to identify an animal all over the world for other scientists. The scientific name is usually made up of two words. The first identifies a genus, or group, of similar animals (or plants), and the second identifies the species, or kind, of animal in the group. Sometimes, as scientists learn more about an animal, they may decide it belongs to a different group. The scientific name is then changed so that all scientists can recognize it and know exactly what animal it refers to.

If you want to learn more about the creatures in this book, the list of scientific names that follows will be useful to you. A typical species has been identified for each type of animal mentioned in the book. There may be other species in the same group.

Chapter	Common Name	Scientific Name
4.	Abalone	*Haliotis fulgeus*
	Anchovy	*Engraulis mordax*
	Bat Star	*Patiria miniata*
	Brittle Star	*Ophioderma panamense*
	California Spiny Lobster	*Panulirus interruptus*
	"Cleaner" Shrimp	*Lysmata californica*
	Convictfish	*Oxylebius pictus*
	Cormorant	*Phalacrocorax penicillatus*
	Garibaldi	*Hypsypops rubicunda*
	Halfmoon	*Medialuna californiensis*
	Harbor Seal	*Phoca vitulina*
	Heron (Great Blue)	*Ardea herodias*
	Hydroid	*Aglaophenia struthenoides*
	Kelpcurler	*Ampithoe humeralis*

Chapter	Common Name	Scientific Name
	Kelp Gribble	*Limnoria algarum*
	Kelp Snail	*Tegula brunnea*
	Mackerel	*Pneumatophorus diego*
	Moray Eel	*Gymnothorax mordax*
	Moss Animal	*Membranipora membranacea*
	Octopus	*Octopus bimaculatus*
	Opaleye	*Girella nigricans*
	Opossum Shrimp	*Acanthomysis sculpta*
	Pelican (Brown)	*Pelecanus occidentalis*
	Pipefish	*Syngnathus leptorhyncus*
	Rock Scallop	*Hinnites multirugosus*
	Sardine	*Sardinia carulea*
	Scorpionfish (Sculpin)	*Scorpeana guttata*
	Sea Lion (California)	*Zalophus californianus*

Chapter	Common Name	Scientific Name
	Sea Otter	Enhydra lutris
	Sea Slug	Flabellinopsis iodinea
	Sea Squirt	Styela montereyensis
	Sea Urchin (Purple)	Strongylocentrotus purpuratus
	Señorita	Oxyjulis californica
	Shovelnose Guitarfish	Rhinobatos productus
	Topsmelt	Atherinops affinis

 *Glossary*

algae (AL-jee)—groups of primitive plants, living mostly in water, that are different from flowering plants living on land. Algae do not have true roots, stems, or leaves, and their sexual structures are very simple

algin (AL-jin)—a natural substance, found in the cell walls of kelp, with a special ability to control large quantities of water

alginates (AL-jih-nates)—various salts manufactured from algin, the sticky substance found in the cell walls of kelp plants

antiseptic (ant-uh-SEP-tik)—a substance that makes whatever it touches so clean that germs cannot grow there

"biological (buy-uh-LAHJ-ih-kuhl) desert"—a region with so few animals and plants that it has almost no nutrients to offer

blade—used here to mean the flat, extended part of a kelp plant that is like the leaf of a plant growing on land

bow—the front end of a ship

canopy (CAN-uh-pee)—the thick upper layer of branches in a forest of giant kelp or a forest of trees on land

carnivore (KAHR-nuh-vohr)—an animal that feeds on the flesh of other animals

cell wall—the firm wall that surrounds and supports a cell, the small basic unit of structure of living things

conveyor (cuhn-VAY-uhr) belts—endless moving belts that carry material from one place to another

crevice (KREV-ihs)—a narrow opening resulting from a split or crack

detritus (dih-TRY-tuhs)—used here to mean bits and pieces of kelp tissue that break apart as a kelp frond dies, providing food for many marine animals

diameter (dy-AM-uh-tuhr)—the length of a straight line through the center of an object

"drapers"—twin conveyor belts that carry kelp cuttings up from the surface of the ocean to the kelp harvester

energy—the ability to be active or to do work; many forms of energy are used to meet human needs

equator—an imaginary line circling the earth at equal distances from the north and south poles

equatorial (ee-kwuh-TOR-ee-uhl)—of, or at, the equator

filter feeders—used here to mean animals that strain particles of food out of seawater

food chain—the connection among living things within a community in nature where larger animals feed upon smaller animals and plants

frond (FRAHND)—used here to mean the part of a kelp plant that is like the branch of a tree growing on land

gamete (GAM-meet)—a mature reproductive cell that can join with another gamete to form a new individual

gel (jel)—a jelly-like state, more solid than liquid

habitat (HAB-uh-tat)—the place where a plant or an animal usually lives

hemisphere (HEHM-uh-sfihr)—half of the globe; the earth has a northern and a southern hemisphere

herbivore (HUR-buh-vohr)—an animal that feeds only on plants

holdfast—the tangle of clinging strands that attaches a kelp plant to a hard surface on the ocean floor

kelp ecosystem (EHK-oh-sis-tuhm)—the total community unit of a kelp bed and the portion of the ocean that is right around it

leaf index—used here to mean the total "leaf" area of a kelp plant, divided by the area of ocean bottom it covers

lift pump—a machine for raising water against the downward pull of gravity

mammal—a warm-blooded animal that nurses its young with milk from the mother's body

marine biologist—a scientist who studies the plant and animal life of the sea

microscopic (my-kro-SCOP-ik)—extremely small in size; an object that can be seen only with a microscope

natural resource—a source of supply of natural materials used to meet human needs

nutrients (NYU-tree-ents)—substances that provide food for living things. Plankton is rich in nutrients

outfall—the outlet of a drain or sewer

parasite (PAHR-uh-site)—a creature often harmful, that lives in or on another creature

photosynthesis (foh-tuh-SIHN-thuh-sihs)—the set of processes that captures the energy of sunlight and uses that energy to convert carbon dioxide and water into sugars. The sugars provide building blocks for the cell and store energy for future use.

plankton—a mass of tiny plants and animals floating in the sea; many are microscopic

pneumatocysts (new-MAT-oh-sists)—the gas-filled bulbs of a kelp plant that serve as floats

polluted (puh-LOOT-ed)—made dirty or impure

potash (PAHT-ash)—a potassium compound, often obtained from ashes, used in agriculture or industry

predator (PREHD-uh-tor)—an animal that kills and eats other animals

prey (PRAY)—an animal hunted by a predator as food

primary stipe (styp)—the main stalk of a kelp plant above the holdfast

reproduce—to produce new individuals of the same kind, by a sexual or asexual (without the union of individuals or germ cells) process

satellite — used here to mean an artificial object which orbits the earth

scimitar (SIM-uh-tuhr) blade—used here to mean the emerging part of a kelp frond that has the curved shape of a saber

sessile (SES-ihl)—permanently attached; not free to move about

species (SPEE-sheez)—distinct kinds of individual plants or animals that have common characteristics and share the same scientific name

spore—used here to mean a primitive single cell produced by a kelp plant for reproduction; the spore will develop into a microscopic plant that will release gametes

sporophylls (SPOR-uh-fihls)—special blades on kelp plants that carry spores

stern—the back end of a ship

stipe (styp)—the central stalk of a kelp frond

substrate (SUHB-strayt)—used here to mean a base to which an encrusting animal or plant attaches itself

tentacles (TEHN-tuh-kuhls)— armlike extensions on the body of a sea animal; used for moving, feeling, or grasping

tidepool—a pool of seawater in which sea creatures are captive until the tide comes in and allows them to leave

tissue (TISH-oo)—a group of similar cells bound together to form one of the structural materials of a plant or animal

topographical (tahp-uh-GRAF-ih-kuhl) — relating to charts or maps showing the position or the height of land features or water levels of a region

trade winds—strong winds blowing steadily toward the equator

translocation (trans-low-KAY-shuhn)—used here to mean the movement of dissolved substances from one part of a plant to another part

trillion—a thousand billion. Written as 1,000,000,000,000

upwelling—a natural upward movement of water from the depths of the ocean near a seacoast

wheelhouse—the protected place on a ship where the captain turns a wheel in order to navigate

zygote (ZY-goht)—used here to mean a cell formed by the union of two gametes; a cell that will grow into a new giant kelp plant

 *Selected Bibliography*

Books

Abbott, I.A. and Hollenberg, G.J. *Marine Algae of California*. Stanford, CA: Stanford University Press, 1976.

Brown, J.E. *Wonders of a Kelp Forest*. New York: Dodd, Mead, 1974.

Calder, Nigel. *The Weather Machine*. New York: Viking, 1975.

Chapman, V.J. *Seaweeds and their Uses*. London: Metheun, 1970.

Cuchlaine, A.M.K. *An Introduction to Oceanography*. New York: McGraw Hill, 1963.

Dawson, E. Yale. *Seashore Plants of Southern California*. Berkeley, CA: University of California Press, 1966.

Duddington, C.L. *Flora of the Sea*. New York: Crowell, 1966.

North, W.J., ed. *The Biology of Giant Kelp Beds (Macrocystis) in California*. Lehre, Germany: Cramer, 1971.

——— . *Underwater California*. Berkeley, CA: University of California Press, 1976.

Ricketts, E.F., Calvin, Jack, and Hedgpeth, J.W. *Between Pacific Tides*. Stanford, CA: Stanford University Press, 1968.

Thorson, Gunnar. *Life in the Sea.* New York: McGraw Hill, 1971.

Waaland, J. Robert. *Common Seaweeds of the Pacific Coast.* Seattle: Pacific Search Press, 1977.

Articles
Ashkenazy, Irvin. "Kelp Farm—Cultivating Energy on Ocean Plantations." *Oceans*, May-June 1981.

Golden, Frederic. "Tracking That Crazy Weather." *Time*, April 11, 1983.

Salters, Richard. "Aquaculture—Wave of the Future." *Science Digest*, June 1981.

 *Index*

abalone, 13, 40, 46
algae, 19, 24, 43, 48
algin, 10, 54-56, 59-61, 69
alginates, 56-59, 60
"biological deserts," 96
blades (kelp), 23, 34, 39, 45
brittle stars, 45
bull kelp, 9
California Current, 32, 84
California spiny lobster, 40
canopy (kelp), 31, 46-47, 62, 68, 69, 90
carnivores, 16, 46
cell walls, 55, 60
chlorophyll, 19, 92
Columbus, Christopher, 48-49
Darwin, Charles, 16-17
detritus, 14, 39, 79
"drapers," 64-65
elk kelp, 9
"El Niño," 83, 86-87, 90-91
equator, 35, 83-84, 86
feather-boa kelp, 9, 34
filter feeders, 14, 16, 39
fronds, 20, 23-24, 30, 31
gametes, 27, 69
garibaldi, 43
gels, 58
giant kelp: color of, 19, 28; destruction of, 73, 77; food chain and, 13-14, 16, 39, 43, 45; food for, 34-35; function of, 47; growing conditions and, 32, 34, 79, 81; harvesting of, 50, 53-54, 56, 59-62, 64-65; location of, 35-36; ocean farms and, 95-96, 100-102; origin of, 49; photosynthesis and, 31; pollution and, 72, 80; products of, 10, 49-52, 53, 55-56, 60-61; reproduction of, 24, 27; size of, 9, 37; structure of, 55; weather and, 87, 90-91
guano, 51-52
herbivores, 14
holdfasts, 20, 24, 40, 96, 100, 101
Hooker, J. D., 49
Humboldt Current, 83, 86
hydroids, 39
iodine, 52-53
kelp beds: canopy of, 31; care of, 60, 70, carnivores and, 16; color of, 10, 28, filter feeders and, 16, 39-40; function of, 9; harvesting of, 62-65, 68-69; kelp ecosystem and, 16, 45-46, 70, 73, 75-55; location of, 53; weather and, 84, 86
Kelco, 56, 60
kelpcurler, 45

kelp ecosystem, 16, 35, 76, 77, 79
kelp farms, 95-96, 102
kelp forests, 28, 30-31, 37, 40, 47, 70, 75
kelp gribble, 40
kelp harvester, 62-65, 68-69
kelps, 48-51, 55, 56
kelp tree house, 37, 40, 42, 47
leaf index, 37
Leighton, Dr. David, 75
moray eel, 40
moss animals, 39
nitrogen, 72
North, Dr. Wheeler, 70, 72, 75, 76-77
Northern Hemisphere, 35, 84, 96
nutrients, 20, 34-35, 70, 72, 83, 86, 96, 101
ocean farms, 92, 95-96, 100-101
opossum shrimp, 39, 40
outfalls, sewer, 70, 72
parasites, 40
Peru Current, 83, 86
photosynthesis, 13, 19, 31, 72, 92
pipefish, 43
plankton, 14, 83
pneumatocysts, 23
pollution, 70, 72
potash, 50, 53
predators, 16, 39, 40, 73, 75, 79
primary stipe, 30, 73

Sargasso Sea, 48-49
scimitar blade, 24
"sea club," 50
sea lions, 46
sea otters, 46, 63-64, 75-77
sea slug, 39
sea urchins, 13, 40, 42, 46, 73, 75-77, 79
seaweed, as food, 48. *See also* giant kelp
señorita, 43
sessile animals, 37, 39
sewage, 70, 72
soda ash, 50-52
solar energy, 13, 92, 95-96
Southern Hemisphere, 35, 84
spores, 24, 27, 102
sporophylls, 24
Stanford, E. C., 55, 61
stipes, 20, 23, 31, 34
substrate, 14, 49
tissues (kelp), 50, 55-56, 59-60, 61
Topographical Explorer (TOP-EX), 91
trade winds, 84, 86, 90
translocation, 31
upwellings, 34-35
Wilcox, Dr. Howard A., 92, 96, 100
zygotes, 27, 69, 102

About the Author

A free-lance writer and former teacher, Mary Daegling first became interested in the giant kelps several years ago when she interviewed Dr. Wheeler J. North of the California Institute of Technology. "When I first interviewed Dr. North," she says, "I had in mind writing only a short article about the kelp beds off the coast of southern California. However, on the way home from that first interview, I realized that the world of kelp was a very interesting one, and that I would like to know more about it. This book is a tribute to the kelp experts who are so generous in sharing their knowledge with others and to the public librarians who helped me obtain many of the books I needed to complete my research on this fascinating subject."

Ms. Daegling is a member of the Society of Children's Book Writers. A graduate of Stanford University, she lives with her husband in San Marino, California. They are the parents of three grown children.